Voices

Of

Success:

Devotional

and Study Guide

For Business Leaders

Voices of Success:

Devotional

And Study Guide

For Business Leaders

First Printing: 2025 Ordering Information:

Special discounts are available on quantity purchases by corporations, associations, educators, and others. For details, contact the publisher at the email listed below.

ISBN: 979-8-9991788-1-7

U.S. trade bookstores and wholesalers:

Please contact coachls.w2r@gmail.com

Dedication

This Devotional and Study Guide is dedicated to you, who has an idea and is willing to step through your fear to make it a reality.

This is one of those ideas that was initiated from a question asked, a fear that was quickly extinguished, and the next step was taken.

You never know what the journey will be like and what will happen when you step through the scary of doing something you have never done before.

Take this and use it as your tool to succeed.

Acknowledgments

Without the phenomenal co-authors in the first book, Voices of Success: from 0 to Six Figures, this one would never have happened.

This book is from those who are ready to answer the tough questions and perhaps some you will never have to answer, or some are for another season of your life.

✪Thank you to Jose Escobar who believes in me to always succeed. You have been my mentor, my coach, and now my friend.

✪Thank you to Dr. Reid for persevering, being a great example of success and faith, and who continues to give me a courage I didn't even know I had.

✪Thank you to Nicky Cuesta. I have watched her grow from the very first podcast and building her own community into a powerful build each other up and don't tear each other down at all sisterhood. Her own life story and ups and downs are inspirational.

Introduction

Welcome to *Devotional Testimonies*—a sacred collection of real stories and raw moments transformed into daily encounters with God. These aren't just journal entries or reflections; they are lived experiences where faith was tested, voices were found, and purpose was revealed.

Each section—shared by Nicky, Dr. Reid, Jose, and LS—offers a unique lens through which to see God's presence: in courage, in darkness, in daily life, and in the tender unfolding of identity. Every devotion includes scripture, thoughtful reflection, and space for journaling—so you can discover how their story helps you uncover your own.

Let their testimonies walk with you. Let them remind you: God is still writing yours.

This devotional is:

- Testimony-driven: Real stories shared with transparency and faith.
- Scripture-anchored: Each devotion includes specific Bible verses to read.
- Reflective: Thoughtful questions guide the reader to apply the themes to their own life.
- Interactive: Journal prompts allow readers to respond personally.

Purpose: To help readers connect with God through the lens of someone else's experience, while also exploring their own.

How to use this devotional

This devotional is in four parts, one for each of the co-authors of the book, _Voices of Success from 0 to Six Figures_. These are taken from the testimonies of the co-authors in the book and will be broken down into daily guides.

There is no right or wrong answer. There may be parts you don't understand or cannot answer at this time because each of us goes through seasons in our lives at different times. What may seem unanswerable today, may in a few months or a few years, become answerable at that time, or perhaps, it may never apply to you. It is all okay.

From OpenSource AI ChatGPT: (which I used for partial editing and formatting)

Testimonies aren't all linear or polished—sometimes they're still unfolding, filled with questions, raw moments, and personal nuance. That's what makes them relatable.

Your depth and transparency offer space for readers who feel "in-between," doubting, or rebuilding faith slowly.

It's not about perfection—it's about presence. God is in the real, the wrestling, the wondering. That's devotional gold.

Prayer Journal Prompts

These are in the back of the book to do on your own, as you feel that you could use a boost for something specific in your life or in the lives of another.

Devotions with Nicky

Don't Wait—Create: The Faith Walk That Funded My
Purpose
By Nicky Cuesta

Day 1: "If Not Now, When?"

Read: Jeremiah 29:11, Hebrews 11:1

Excerpt:

"There's something sacred about stillness… I didn't have all the answers. But I had a calling. And I had a choice."

Reflect:

When was the last time you were still enough to hear God's whisper?

_____

_____

_____

What choice have you been avoiding because it feels too uncertain?

_____

_____

_____

Study Insight: Jeremiah 29:11 reminds us that God has a plan, even when we feel uncertain. Hebrews 11:1 defines faith as confidence in what we hope for and assurance about what we do not see. Faith doesn't require the full picture—only a willing step forward.

Personal Application: Write a short prayer or declaration about something you are stepping into, even without having all the answers. What is God asking you to trust Him with today?

Journal: Write a short prayer or reflection about a time you heard God calling you to something new.

_____

_____

_____

_____

_____

_____

_____

_____

_____

_____

_____

_____

_____

_____

_____

_____

_____

_____

_____

_____

Day 2: "From Chicago to Philly—Faith in the Unknown"

Read: Genesis 12:1, Isaiah 43:19

Excerpt:

"I left behind familiarity, a long-term relationship, and a steady job... but I knew I was ready for more."

Reflect:

What's your "Philly" moment—when did you follow faith into the unknown?

_____

_____

_____

What prepared you for a change you didn't expect?

_____

_____

_____

How has God shown you new things when you left your comfort zone?

_____

_____

Study Insight: In Genesis 12, God called Abram to leave everything familiar for a promise he couldn't yet see. Isaiah 43:19 reminds us that God makes a way—even in wilderness seasons. Stepping out is not about certainty, but about obedience.

Personal Application: Describe an area where God may be calling you to leave behind comfort to pursue something greater. Write a prayer asking for courage and vision to walk forward.

Journal: Describe a moment when stepping away from comfort led to growth.

_____

_____

_____

_____

_____

_____

_____

_____

_____

_____

_____

_____

_____

_____

_____

_____

_____

_____

_____

Day 3: "Climbing, but Questioning"

Read: Colossians 3:23, Galatians 1:10

Excerpt:

"That's the thing about imposter syndrome: it doesn't care how good you are; it cares how worthy you believe you are."

Reflect:

Have you ever questioned your worth, even when you were succeeding?

_____

_____

_____

What daily practice helps you refill when you're pouring into others?

_____

_____

_____

What can you do to keep showing up when you feel unseen or undervalued?

_____

_____

Study Insight: Colossians 3:23 calls us to work as though we're serving the Lord, not man. Galatians 1:10 reminds us that seeking approval from people can hinder us from fully following Christ. Our worth isn't determined by our title—it's rooted in our Creator.

Personal Application: Write a statement of truth about your identity in Christ. What lies are you replacing today with God's truth about your value?

Journal: What truths about your worth can you hold onto today?

_____

_____

_____

_____

_____

_____

_____

_____

_____

_____

_____

_____

_____

_____

_____

_____

_____

_____

_____

_____

_____

Day 4: "The Breaking Point and the Call"

Read: 1 Kings 19:11-13, Psalm 46:10

Excerpt:

"That's when I heard it. Clear as day: 'If not now, when?'"

Reflect:

Have you experienced a breaking point that became a turning point? If so, what was it?

_____

_____

_____

What question has God asked you in this season?

_____

_____

_____

Study Insight: In 1 Kings 19, God met Elijah not in the wind, earthquake, or fire—but in a gentle whisper. Psalm 46:10 calls us to be still and know. Sometimes, the most powerful direction comes in the quiet moments after we've been emptied of everything else.

Personal Application: Reflect on a time when you reached your limit. How did God meet you there? Write a prayer of surrender or recommitment to His voice.

Journal: Write a response to God's call on your heart right now.

_____

_____

_____

_____

_____

_____

_____

_____

_____

_____

_____

_____

_____

_____

_____

_____

_____

_____

_____

_____

Day 5: "The Birth of a Movement"

Read: Habakkuk 2:2-3, Romans 12:6-8

Excerpt:

"I launched BALM GLOBAL in faith... No blueprint. No investor. Just belief."

Reflect:

What have you built or launched by faith?

_____

_____

_____

What part of your story could be the beginning of someone else's breakthrough?

_____

_____

_____

What community or legacy are you being led to create?

_____

_____

Study Insight: Habakkuk reminds us to write the vision and wait for its appointed time—it will not delay. Paul's words in Romans show us that each person's gift is unique and essential. Movements begin not with permission, but with obedience.

Personal Application: Write down a vision God has placed in your heart. What's one step you can take this week to act on it by faith?

Journal: What dream do you need to put on paper today?

_____

_____

_____

_____

_____

_____

_____

_____

_____

_____

_____

_____

_____

_____

_____

_____

_____

_____

_____

Day 6: "Every Yes Unlocks"

Read: James 2:17, Proverbs 3:5-6

Excerpt:

"Every yes unlocked a new version of me. Not because I was ready, but because I was willing."

Reflect:

What opportunities might God be waiting for you to say yes to?

_____

_____

_____

Where are you being invited to lead?

_____

_____

_____

Have you experienced growth simply by saying yes before you felt fully prepared?

_____

_____

Study Insight: James 2:17 reminds us that faith without works is dead. Proverbs 3:5–6 teaches us to trust in the Lord and submit to Him, and He will make our paths straight. Saying yes is the beginning of walking in God's plan—even without full clarity.

Personal Application: Identify one area where God is asking for your yes. Write a declaration of obedience, even if it feels uncomfortable or uncertain.

Journal: What does bold obedience look like in your life?

_____

_____

_____

_____

_____

_____

_____

_____

_____

_____

_____

_____

_____

_____

_____

_____

_____

_____

_____

_____

_____

Day 7: "Legacy & the Mirror"

Read: Psalm 139:14, 2 Timothy 4:7-8

Excerpt:

"I didn't let statistics, systems, or self-doubt stop me. I still battle the inner hater... but I've learned to fight back."

Reflect:

What legacy are you building through your obedience and courage with your story?

_____

_____

_____

What would your reflection say back to you today?

_____

_____

_____

Study Insight: Psalm 139:14 affirms we are fearfully and wonderfully made. 2 Timothy 4 encourages us to finish our race faithfully. Romans 8 reminds us that nothing can separate us from God's love—not failure, not fear, not even our inner critic.

Personal Application: Write a letter to the woman in the mirror. Speak life, truth, and legacy over her. Remind her she is equipped and enough.

Journal: Speak life to the woman in the mirror—write her a letter.

_____

_____

_____

_____

_____

_____

_____

_____

_____

_____

_____

_____

_____

_____

_____

_____

_____

_____

_____

Faith Insight from Nicky's devotions.

- Understanding our identity in Christ empowers us to lead with confidence. We are not defined by our past but by who God says we are.

- Faith is the antidote to fear. By trusting in God's promises, we can move forward boldly, even when the path is uncertain.

- Vulnerability is not a weakness but a strength. It allows us to connect deeply with others and demonstrates our reliance on God's grace.

- Integrity is the cornerstone of effective leadership. When our actions align with our values, we build trust and reflect Christ's character.

- Jesus exemplified servant leadership. By putting others' needs before our own, we lead with humility and make a lasting impact.

- Change is inevitable, but with God's guidance, we can navigate transitions gracefully, trusting that He is working all things for our good.

- Gratitude shifts our focus from what's lacking to God's abundant blessings, fostering joy and contentment in every season.

- Encouragement uplifts and inspires. By speaking life into others, we help them see their potential and God's purpose for their lives.

- Trials test our faith but also strengthen it. Perseverance through challenges refines our character and deepens our dependence on God.

- Generosity reflects God's heart. When we give freely, we participate in His work and experience the joy of blessing others.

- Wisdom is more than knowledge; it's applying God's truth to our lives. Seeking His guidance leads to sound decisions and fruitful outcomes.

- Prayer is our direct line to God. It's through consistent communication with Him that we gain clarity, peace, and strength for the journey.

- Living purposefully means aligning our daily actions with God's calling. When we do, our lives become a testament to His glory.

Devotions with Dr. Reid

When God Met Me in the Dark (Extended Edition)
By Dr. Oliver T. Reid

Day 1: "The Closet Was My Cocoon"

Scripture to Read: Romans 8:28, Genesis 50:20

Testimony Excerpt:

"These early moments were not merely traumatic; they were formative. Pain became a teacher. Darkness became a classroom."

Reflection Questions:

Have you experienced a time when darkness became your teacher?

_____

_____

_____

How has God used your pain to form your purpose?

_____

_____

_____

Study Insight: Romans 8:28 assures us that all things work together for good to those who love God. Genesis 50:20 echoes this—what was meant for harm, God can use for good. God doesn't waste your pain—He transforms it.

Personal Application: Write a reflection on a painful experience and how God has (or might still) use it for His purpose.

Journal: What fear or identity struggle from childhood still lingers? How do you want God to rewrite it? Ask God to reframe it with His truth.

_____

_____

_____

_____

_____

_____

_____

_____

_____

_____

_____

_____

_____

_____

_____

_____

_____

_____

_____

_____

_____

Day 2: "Developed in the Dark"

Scripture to Read: Isaiah 45:3, Psalm 139:11–12

Testimony Excerpt:

"Every great picture is developed in a darkroom. I had to be processed in a way that couldn't be done in public view."

Reflection Questions:

What have you learned in your hidden seasons?

_____

_____

_____

How might God be developing you now, even if no one sees it?

_____

_____

_____

Study Insight: Isaiah 45:3 speaks of treasures hidden in darkness. Psalm 139 reminds us that even the dark is not dark to God. The hidden places are often where God does His most important work in us.

Personal Application: Journal about something you are currently going through that feels hidden. What might God be forming in you there?

Journal: What three lessons has pain taught you that reshaped your direction or outlook? Pray and thank God for growth in unexpected places.

_____

_____

_____

_____

_____

_____

_____

_____

_____

_____

_____

_____

_____

_____

_____

_____

Day 3: "When Samuel's Voice Found Me"

Scripture to Read: 1 Samuel 3:1–10, John 10:27

Testimony Excerpt:

"She advised me to respond, 'Speak, Lord, for your servant is listening.'... I was being summoned even before I understood the weight."

Reflection Questions:

Have you ever sensed God calling you before you felt ready?

_____

_____

_____

How do you tune your heart to recognize His voice?

_____

_____

_____

Study Insight: 1 Samuel 3 shows that even the young and unsure can be called by God. John 10:27 affirms that God's sheep know His voice. Sometimes, the call precedes our confidence.

Personal Application: Write a short prayer asking God to help you recognize His voice clearly, especially in seasons of uncertainty.

Journal: Where in your life do you feel hidden right now? What fruit might God be forming there?

_____

_____

_____

_____

_____

_____

_____

_____

_____

_____

_____

_____

_____

_____

_____

_____

_____

_____

_____

_____

_____

Day 4: "Marked from the Beginning"

Scripture to Read: Jeremiah 1:5, Ephesians 2:10

Testimony Excerpt:

"The enemy doesn't attack what isn't a threat... My early life was met with opposition because hell saw the potential in me before I did."

Reflection Questions:

How have early struggles pointed toward your calling?

_____

_____

_____

Where might you need to reframe your past as preparation?

_____

_____

_____

Study Insight: Jeremiah 1:5 tells us God knew us before we were born. Ephesians 2:10 reminds us we were created for good works prepared in advance. Opposition is often confirmation of purpose.

Personal Application: List a few challenges you faced early in life. Write how they may have been training ground for your assignment.

Journal: After sitting in silence, what did you hear, feel, or realize? Write it as if God is speaking directly to you. Write down what you sense

_____

_____

_____

_____

_____

_____

_____

_____

_____

_____

_____

_____

_____

_____

_____

_____

_____

_____

_____

_____

_____

_____

Day 5: "A Pivotal Christmas"

Scripture to Read: Psalm 34:18, Isaiah 61:3
Testimony Excerpt:

"On the outside, people may have seen a young man going through a hard time. But inside, I was raging."

Reflection Questions:

What pain have you hidden from others?

_____

_____

_____

Where has God brought beauty from your ashes?

_____

_____

_____

Study Insight: Psalm 34:18 promises that God is near to the brokenhearted. Isaiah 61:3 reminds us that He gives beauty for ashes, joy for mourning, and praise for despair.

Personal Application: Write a letter to God sharing your honest feelings from a low point in your life. Invite Him into the healing process.

Journal: Where has adversity revealed your assignment? How can you begin to own that calling today

_____

_____

_____

_____

_____

_____

_____

_____

_____

_____

_____

_____

_____

_____

_____

_____

_____

_____

_____

_____

_____

_____

Day 6: "God Interrupted My Exit Plan"

Scripture to Read: Lamentations 3:22–23, Psalm 18:16

Testimony Excerpt:

"There were no words—just a weighty peace... That moment became an altar."

Reflection Questions:

When has God met you at your lowest moment?

_____

_____

_____

How has His presence changed your perspective?

_____

_____

_____

Study Insight: Lamentations assures us of new mercies every morning. Psalm 18:16 speaks of a God who rescues us when we're sinking. Sometimes He answers with peace, not explanation.

Personal Application: Write about a time God's peace found you. Describe how it changed your direction or outlook.

Journal: Write a letter to God from the depths of your past pain. Then write His response back to you.

_____

_____

_____

_____

_____

_____

_____

_____

_____

_____

_____

_____

_____

_____

_____

_____

_____

_____

_____

_____

_____

_____

Day 7: "Pain Is Not Pointless"

Scripture to Read: Romans 5:3–5, James 1:2–4

Testimony Excerpt:

"He didn't erase the trauma. He repurposed it."

Reflection Questions:

What pain has God repurposed in your life?

_____

_____

_____

Where have you grown stronger because of suffering?

_____

_____

_____

Study Insight: Romans and James both teach that suffering produces endurance, character, and hope. God doesn't ask us to ignore pain—He transforms it.

Personal Application: Reflect on a hardship that has deepened your faith. Thank God for how He is using it.

Journal: What hardship has deepened your faith or leadership? How is God using that pain to prepare or position you today?

_____

_____

_____

_____

_____

_____

_____

_____

_____

_____

_____

_____

_____

_____

_____

_____

_____

_____

_____

_____

Day 8: "Ordered Steps, Even in Darkness"

Scripture to Read: Psalm 37:23, Proverbs 16:9

Testimony Excerpt:

"He ordered the steps that led me into the closet—and the steps that led me out."

Reflection Questions:

How has God led you through unexpected seasons?

_____

_____

_____

Do you trust His direction even when it doesn't make sense?

_____

_____

_____

Study Insight: Psalm 37 and Proverbs 16 remind us that while we make plans, God directs our steps. His leading often includes detours that develop us.

Personal Application: Write a prayer of trust for your current path, even if it's uncertain.

Journal: Look back over the last 5 years. Where do you now see that God was ordering your steps—even when you didn't realize it?

_____

_____

_____

_____

_____

_____

_____

_____

_____

_____

_____

_____

_____

_____

_____

_____

_____

_____

Day 9: "From Surviving to Reemerging"

Scripture to Read: John 11:43–44, Ezekiel 37:5–6

Testimony Excerpt:

"I felt like Lazarus being called out of the tomb... I was reemerging."

Reflection Questions:

What part of your life feels like it's being resurrected?

_____

_____

_____

How does God breathe new life into your dry places?

_____

_____

_____

What steps in your life seemed aimless but were actually ordered?

_____

_____

_____

How has God used unexpected paths to direct your purpose?

_____

_____

_____

Study Insight: Jesus called Lazarus forth from the grave. Ezekiel prophesied life to dry bones. Your reemergence is not a surprise—it's a calling.

Personal Application: Write a declaration over a part of your life that is being revived.

Journal: What are you hearing God say to the part of you that's been stuck, silent, or numb? What might it look like to come forth and walk again?_____

_____

_____

_____

_____

_____

_____

_____

_____

_____

_____

_____

_____

_____

_____

_____

_____

_____

_____

Day 10: "The Call on Youth"

Scripture to Read: 1 Timothy 4:12, Jeremiah 1:6–8

Testimony Excerpt:

"Being young doesn't exempt you from pain. It often makes you a target."

Reflection Questions:

What limitations have others put on you that God has not?

_____

_____

_____

How can you encourage the next generation through your story?

_____

_____

_____

Study Insight: 1 Timothy and Jeremiah show us that age doesn't disqualify you. God chooses and equips regardless of experience.

Personal Application: Write a note to your younger self, filled with encouragement and affirmation.

Journal: What painful or overlooked chapter in your youth still impacts how you lead or love today? What might God be redeeming through it?

_____

_____

_____

_____

_____

_____

_____

_____

_____

_____

_____

_____

_____

_____

_____

_____

_____

_____

_____

Day 11: "The Gift of Discernment"

Scripture to Read: Hebrews 5:14, Proverbs 2:6–9

Testimony Excerpt:

"The closet gave me discernment... It birthed a spiritual radar."

Reflection Questions:

How has hardship sharpened your discernment?

_____

_____

_____

What can your sensitivity to others teach the Church? [the Church is the people not the building]

_____

_____

_____

Study Insight: Discernment is forged through practice and pain. God refines our spiritual instincts through real experience.

Personal Application: Ask God to heighten your discernment today. Reflect on how He has already grown your spiritual awareness.

Journal: When have you sensed something others missed? How might your ability to "read the room" be a gift God wants to use more intentionally?

_____

_____

_____

_____

_____

_____

_____

_____

_____

_____

_____

_____

_____

_____

_____

_____

_____

_____

_____

Day 12: "From Pain to Preaching"

Scripture to Read: 2 Corinthians 1:3–4, Isaiah 61:1

Testimony Excerpt:

"I don't preach to entertain—I preach to rescue."

Reflection Questions:

What part of your pain can bring hope to someone else?

_____

_____

_____

How has God used your story to minister?

_____

_____

_____

Study Insight: God comforts us so we can comfort others. Our healing is part of our mission.

Personal Application: Write about someone you feel called to help—and how your story might be the key.

Journal: What part of your story might God be asking you to share with someone else? How has your pain positioned you to lead with empathy and authority?

_____

_____

_____

_____

_____

_____

_____

_____

_____

_____

_____

_____

_____

_____

_____

_____

_____

_____

Day 13: "Following the Light Trail"

Scripture to Read: Psalm 119:105, Psalm 139:12

Testimony Excerpt:

"If you trace the steps of what you've been through in the dark, it leads to light rooms."

Reflection Questions:

What has your journey through darkness revealed?

_____

_____

_____

How do you know God has guided your path?

_____

_____

_____

How has God used your pain to illuminate a path for others?

_____

_____

_____

Study Insight: God's Word lights the path. His presence brings clarity even when the trail is dim.

Personal Application: Draw a timeline of your life's darkest and brightest moments. Mark where God met you.

Journal: As you look back, what "light trail" has emerged from your darkest moments? How does it guide you now?

_____

_____

_____

_____

_____

_____

_____

_____

_____

_____

_____

_____

_____

_____

_____

_____

_____

_____

_____

_____

_____

Day 14: "What the Darkness Couldn't Do"

Scripture to Read: Romans 8:38–39, John 1:5

Testimony Excerpt:

"What felt like rejection was redirection... what felt like darkness was development."

Reflection Questions:

What couldn't the enemy steal from you?

_____

_____

_____

What was formed in you that only darkness could produce?

_____

_____

_____

Study Insight: God's love is unshakable. Even the darkest moments can't dim His light or rewrite His plan.

Personal Application: Write a praise of victory: what did the darkness fail to defeat in your life?

Journal: Declare what the darkness could not do to you. Speak and write what it couldn't stop, silence, or steal. Let that become your praise.

Faith Insight from Dr. Reids devotions.

- Even if others mislabel or abandon you, God never will. He is present in every dark place—redeeming what others tried to ruin.

- The lessons that shape destiny are often born from the hardest classrooms. God doesn't waste pain—He works through it.

- God uses hidden seasons to prepare us for revealed purpose. Where you feel buried, you may actually be planted.

- What tried to take you out may have only confirmed what you were born to do. Attacks are often prophetic clues to your purpose.

- Pain does not disprove God's presence—it reveals how deeply He pursues us in silence.

- Both Romans and James teach that suffering produces endurance, character, and hope. God doesn't ask us to ignore pain—He transforms it.

- God doesn't just guide the glorious moments—He orders every uncertain, silent, even painful step. Trust is not built by clarity but by commitment to follow.

- The voice of Jesus doesn't just comfort the wounded—it awakens the sleeping. What felt like the end might just be the beginning of your reemergence.

- Throughout Scripture, God chooses young people to carry bold assignments—often after seasons of rejection, misunderstanding, or pain. If your beginnings were hard, your future may be holy.

- Spiritual discernment is often sharpened in isolation and adversity. It is not merely the ability to perceive truth, but to respond with wisdom and compassion shaped by experience.

- Ministry is born in the places you've bled. You're not called to impress the crowd but to reach the one who's still in the dark. When your purpose flows from your pain, your voice carries power.

- Nothing is wasted with God—not even the shadows. He transforms isolation into illumination and turns your trials into trails of testimony.

- The enemy can try to delay your growth, but he cannot deny God's plan. What the darkness couldn't do—stop your calling—only proves the light within you is real and relentless.

Devotions with Jose

My Faith
By Jose Escobar

Day 1: "Faith at the Forefront"

Read: Proverbs 3:5–6, Colossians 3:17

Excerpt:

"I keep it at the forefront of mind... I always have the Lord present. I say an internal private prayer in my mind before I do anything."

Reflect:

What would it look like to keep God present in all your daily decisions?

_____

_____

_____

How do you bring your faith into your professional life?

_____

_____

_____

In what daily routines or moments do you invite God's presence?

_____

_____

_____

How does prayer shift your mindset in business and life?

_____

_____

_____

Study Insight: Colossians 3:17 reminds us to do everything—word or deed—in Jesus' name. Proverbs 16:3 promises that if we commit our actions to the Lord, our plans will succeed. When we partner with God in the everyday, He guides the outcome.

Personal Application: Write a prayer you can say before meetings or tasks that invites God into the moment. Reflect on how your faith shapes your decisions.

Journal: Write about a moment when your faith shaped the outcome of your day.

_____

_____

_____

_____

_____

_____

_____

_____

_____

_____

_____

_____

_____

_____

_____

_____

_____

_____

_____

_____

_____

Day 2: "A Calling to Impact"

Read: Matthew 5:14–16, Ephesians 2:10

Excerpt:

"I feel called to create massive impact in the world. I feel called to serve people at a very high level, and ultimately around my faith."

Reflect:

What kind of impact do you feel called to create?

_____

_____

_____

How does your faith influence your purpose?

_____

_____

_____

What does "massive impact" mean in your current season?

_____

_____

_____

How does your faith shape the way you serve others?

_____

_____

_____

Study Insight: Matthew 5 reminds us we are the light of the world—we're meant to shine and reflect God's goodness in all we do. Ephesians 2:10 declares that we are God's handiwork, created for good works. Living by faith isn't just personal—it's purposeful.

Personal Application: Write down one way you can serve or lead others this week that reflects God's love and truth. Ask Him to guide your actions for Kingdom impact.

Journal: Describe the connection between your calling and your personal faith walk.

_____

_____

_____

_____

_____

_____

_____

_____

_____

_____

_____

_____

_____

_____

_____

_____

_____

_____

Day 3: "Unapologetic Faith"

Read: Romans 1:16, 1 Peter 3:15

Excerpt:

"I never force my faith onto people, but I'm definitely not shy or afraid of where I stand in my views."

Reflect:

How can you boldly share your faith without forcing it on others?

_____

_____

_____

What helps you stay confident in your beliefs?

_____

_____

_____

When have you boldly expressed your beliefs without apology?

_____

_____

_____

What does it look like to share faith with gentleness and respect?

_____

_____

_____

Study Insight: Romans 1:16 calls us to be unashamed of the Gospel—it is God's power for salvation. 1 Peter 3:15 urges us to always be ready to explain our hope, but to do it with gentleness and respect. Our confidence in Christ doesn't need to be loud to be powerful.

Personal Application: Write a declaration of where you stand in your faith. How will you reflect your beliefs this week with clarity and compassion?

Journal: Reflect on a time when you stood firm in your faith in a public or professional setting.

_____

_____

_____

_____

_____

_____

_____

_____

_____

_____

_____

_____

_____

_____

_____

_____

_____

_____

_____

_____

_____

Day 4: "Faith with a Family"

Read: Joshua 24:15, Ecclesiastes 4:12

Excerpt:

"Our marriage is a marriage of three—God, my wife, and myself. It's the center of our home, in how I parent as well."

Reflect:

How does your faith influence your role in your family?

_____

_____

_____

What role does your faith play in your family relationships?

_____

_____

_____

In what ways can you make God more visible in your home?

_____

_____

_____

How can you bring God's presence more visibly into your home?

_____

_____

_____

Study Insight: Joshua 24:15 is a powerful declaration of choosing to serve the Lord as a household. Ecclesiastes 4:12 reminds us that a cord of three strands is not easily broken. When God is at the center, relationships are strengthened.

Personal Application: Write a prayer over your family—your spouse, children, or future home. How can you lead spiritually in your household this week?

Journal: Write a prayer for your marriage or family that invites God more deeply into your daily life.

_____

_____

_____

_____

_____

_____

_____

_____

_____

_____

_____

_____

_____

_____

_____

_____

_____

_____

_____

_____

_____

Day 5: "Faith Is My Foundation"

Read: Psalm 127:1, Matthew 7:24–25

Excerpt:

"It's part of my fabric; it's part of who I am and what I do. Faith is directly related to my business."

Reflect:

What areas of your life naturally reflect your faith?

_____

_____

_____

Where in your life is faith most integrated? Where is it least?

_____

_____

_____

How can you continue to align your work with your spiritual values?

_____

_____

_____

Are there any areas where faith needs to become more foundational?

_____

_____

_____

Study Insight: Psalm 127:1 reminds us that unless the Lord builds the house, the builders labor in vain. Matthew 6:33 urges us to seek God's Kingdom first—then everything else will fall into place. When faith is woven into the fabric of our lives, everything aligns under His purpose.

Personal Application: Reflect on one area of your life—business, finances, health, relationships—where you want to bring God's guidance to the forefront. What's one faith-driven step you can take?

-

Journal: Describe what it means for faith to be your foundation in business and life.

_____

_____

_____

_____

_____

_____

_____

_____

_____

_____

_____

_____

_____

_____

_____

_____

_____

_____

_____

_____

Faith Insight from Jose's devotions.

- Reflecting on God's faithfulness fuels our gratitude and strengthens our resolve. Celebrating His work in our lives encourages us to continue leading with purpose.
- Our leadership leaves a lasting impact. By focusing on eternal values and investing in others, we build legacies that honor God and inspire future generations.
- Leading with faith is not just a practice—it's a posture. When we invite God into our daily work, decisions, and conversations through constant communion, we align our business and leadership with divine wisdom. Prayer isn't our last resort; it's our first response.
- God's purpose for your life isn't small—it's strategic. When you root your desire to serve in faith, your impact multiplies beyond results into legacy. Faith doesn't just guide your actions—it ignites your mission.
- When God is at the center of our relationships, we lead our homes with purpose and peace. Spiritual leadership begins in the family. The way we love and serve at home reflects the depth of our faith in action.
- Faith isn't something we turn on and off—it flows through every interaction when it's woven into our identity. As believers and leaders, we represent Christ not just in worship, but in every handshake, meeting, and moment.
- Faith isn't an accessory to success—it's the foundation. When your business and leadership are built with God at the center, excellence and impact follow. Faith-driven leaders don't just build profit— they build purpose.
- When you stay connected to the Source, you lead from a place of strength the world can't replicate.

Devotions with LS

My Testimony
By LS Kirkpatrick

Day 1: "The Hand Raised"

Read: 2 Corinthians 5:17, Mark 10:14–15

Excerpt:

"Each night, the same thing repeated, and each night I raised my hand."

Reflect:

What does it mean to you to become a "new creation"?

_____

_____

_____

Have you ever longed for transformation you didn't feel right away?

_____

_____

_____

Study Insight: 2 Corinthians 5:17 reveals the power of new life in Christ—old things pass away, and new things come. Mark 10:14–15 reminds us to approach the kingdom of God like a child: eager, trusting, and open.

Personal Application: Write about a time you wanted to be different or better and how God met you in that longing. What does a fresh start in your faith look like today?

-

Journal: Write about a time you wanted to change and how you kept showing up in faith.

_____

_____

_____

_____

_____

_____

_____

_____

_____

_____

_____

_____

_____

_____

_____

_____

_____

_____

_____

Day 2: "I Do Understand"

Read: 1 Corinthians 2:10–12, Matthew 18:2–4, John 3:3–8, Romans 10:9–10

Excerpt:

"I couldn't take it anymore. I exploded with, 'I do understand!'"

Reflect:

What moments from childhood have shaped your understanding of God?

_____

_____

_____

How have you responded when others questioned your spiritual maturity?

_____

_____

_____

Have you ever questioned your salvation or whether it was "real" enough?

_____

_____

_____

How do you define true change in your spiritual life?

_____

_____

_____

Study Insight: Jesus said we must be born again to see the Kingdom of God. That transformation isn't always felt immediately but is deeply spiritual and enduring. Romans 10 reminds us that belief in the heart and confession with the mouth brings salvation.

Personal Application: Reflect on your salvation story. What made it real to you? Write a short prayer thanking God for His patience as you came to understand His love more fully.

Journal: Write a letter to your younger self affirming your early faith.

_____

_____

_____

_____

_____

_____

_____

_____

_____

_____

_____

_____

_____

_____

_____

_____

_____

_____

_____

_____

Day 3: "When the Preacher Came"

Read: Romans 10:9–10, John 3:3–6, Ezekiel 36:26–27, Galatians 2:20

Excerpt:

"That change I felt was becoming permanent inside me... I knew I was that new creation!"

Reflect:

When did you first feel the presence of God settle within you?

_____

_____

_____

How did that moment change your identity?

_____

_____

_____

What does spiritual transformation feel like for you?

_____

_____

_____

What old patterns or mindsets have passed away since you said yes to Jesus?

_____

_____

_____

Study Insight: Ezekiel speaks of God giving us a new heart and spirit, replacing the old. Galatians 2:20 declares that we've been crucified with Christ and now live by faith in Him. A true transformation often begins with a deep internal shift—even before outward change is visible.

Personal Application: Write a journal entry from your "new creation" self. Who are you becoming in Christ? What has He freed you from—and what is He leading you into?

Journal: Describe the first time you recognized God was truly with you.

_____

_____

_____

_____

_____

_____

_____

_____

_____

_____

_____

_____

_____

_____

_____

_____

_____

_____

_____

_____

Day 4: "Speak Life to Yourself"

Read: Proverbs 18:21, Philippians 4:8

Testimonial Excerpt:

"Say nice things to you. Think great things about you. Be kind to you."

Reflect:

What is the tone of your inner voice lately?

_____

_____

_____

How can your words shape your self-view and your future?

_____

_____

_____

Have you ever hesitated to share a spiritual experience out of fear of disbelief?

_____

_____

_____

What does it mean to trust God with your story?

_____

_____

_____

Study Insight: Jesus promised the Holy Spirit would come to dwell in believers—John 14 calls Him the Comforter and Spirit of Truth. Acts 2 declares that God pours out His Spirit on all people. Your testimony may be the encouragement someone else needs to believe.

Personal Application: Write about a moment when you saw or sensed something divine. What message might God have wanted you to carry from that encounter? How will you share it with courage?

Journal: List five truths about yourself based on God's Word and your growth.

_____

_____

_____

_____

_____

_____

_____

_____

_____

_____

_____

_____

_____

_____

_____

_____

_____

_____

_____

Day 5: "The Way You Treat You"

Read: Luke 10:27, Psalm 139:13–14

Testimonial Excerpt:

"The way you behave to yourself, is the way others will behave to you."

Reflect:

In what ways do you need to model self-respect to others?

_____

_____

_____

How can your treatment of yourself reflect God's love for you?

_____

_____

_____

How do you treat yourself mentally, emotionally, and spiritually?

_____

_____

_____

Do you believe your actions toward yourself reflect how God sees you?

_____

_____

_____

Study Insight: Luke 10:27 teaches us to love our neighbors *as ourselves*—implying we must first love ourselves well. Psalm 139 reminds us that we are fearfully and wonderfully made. God's love for us sets the standard for how we should see and treat ourselves.

Personal Application: Write a few kind, truthful affirmations about yourself today based on how God sees you. How can you show yourself grace and love the way God does?

Journal: Write a prayer asking for help to love and treat yourself as God would.

_____

_____

_____

_____

_____

_____

_____

_____

_____

_____

_____

_____

_____

_____

_____

_____

_____

_____

_____

_____

_____

Day 6: "Look for the Lovely"

Read: Lamentations 3:22–23, Isaiah 43:19

Testimonial Excerpt:

"Every day something wonderful, or amazing, or lovely... is going to happen, so look for it."

Reflect:

What are three beautiful things you noticed today?

_____

_____

_____

How does looking for good change your day?

_____

_____

_____

Are you intentionally looking for God's goodness each day?

_____

_____

_____

How do you train your heart and mind to recognize His new mercies?

_____

_____

_____

Study Insight: Lamentations 3:22–23 promises that God's mercies are new every morning. Isaiah 43:19 reminds us that He is always doing something new—even when we don't perceive it right away. Looking for beauty in the ordinary opens our eyes to divine presence.

Personal Application: Start a gratitude journal. Each morning or evening, write down something beautiful or encouraging that you noticed. Ask God to sharpen your awareness of His daily wonders.

Journal: Keep a short "delight list" for today. Celebrate what is good.

_____

_____

_____

_____

_____

_____

_____

_____

_____

_____

_____

_____

_____

_____

_____

_____

_____

_____

_____

_____

Day 7: "You Are Enough"

Read: Ephesians 2:10, Psalm 8:4–5

Testimonial Excerpt:

"You have great value in you. You are worthy. You are enough. You do matter."

Reflect:

Do you believe these things about yourself?

_____

_____

_____

What evidence in your life confirms your worth and value?

_____

_____

_____

What messages have shaped your beliefs about your worth?

_____

_____

_____

How do God's words redefine what makes you valuable?

_____

_____

_____

Study Insight: Ephesians 2:10 reminds us we are God's masterpiece, created for a purpose. Psalm 8 beautifully expresses God's deep care for humanity—crowned with glory and honor. Your worth isn't earned by achievements; it's affirmed by the Creator who made you.

Personal Application: List the truths God speaks over you from these verses. Which one do you need to believe more deeply today? Declare it aloud and carry it with you.

Journal: Affirm each statement: "I have great value." "I am worthy." "I am enough." "I do matter." Then write why.

_____

_____

_____

_____

_____

_____

_____

_____

_____

_____

_____

_____

_____

_____

_____

_____

_____

_____

_____

_____

Faith Insight from LS's devotions.

- Salvation is both simple and sacred. When a child raises their hand in faith, heaven sees it. God's transformation begins the moment we say "yes," even before we fully understand the how.

- God honors our understanding, no matter our age. Faith isn't proven by age or eloquence—it's revealed in the sincerity of our hearts. When we know Him, even as children, He confirms it with peace.

- . Salvation is a divine exchange. When we surrender our hearts, God doesn't just visit us—He indwells us. That inward confirmation, that unshakable joy, is the mark of a new creation.

- The words we speak shape the world we live in. When we align our self-talk with God's truth, we step into healing, wholeness, and strength. Life and death really are in the power of the tongue—especially when speaking to ourselves.

- Loving your neighbor starts with loving yourself. When you treat yourself as God's beloved creation, you set the tone for how others treat you and how you show up in the world.

- God's goodness is woven into each day. Sometimes you must pause and look with expectation to see the beauty He's placed before you. Hope is sustained by the discipline of noticing His hand.

- Your worth isn't earned—it's declared by God. You are made in His image, designed for good works, and crowned with glory. In Him, you are already enough.

- When you speak truth—even softly—it plants seeds that can bloom in someone else's breakthrough. Your voice, especially when rooted in God's Word, has the power to shape atmospheres and call forth healing.

- Joy isn't based on perfect circumstances; it's rooted in God's presence. Choosing joy is choosing to believe that even in hardship, God is still good—and still working all things together for your good.

- You don't have to be perfect to be powerful. God's grace bridges every gap between where you are and where He's leading you. In your weakness, His strength shines brightest.

Let your light shine bright. You are not here by accident.

You are living proof that God meets us even in the ordinary—
and creates something extraordinary.

These verses remind us that we are chosen, loved, pursued, and treasured by God. He rejoices over us, sacrificed for us, and calls us by name. Our worth is not earned—it is given.

Read: then write out what God says about who you are

- *Ephesians 2:10*

God reminds me that I am _____

_____

- *Psalm 8:4–5*

God reminds me that I am _____

_____

- *Isaiah 43:1–4*

God reminds me that I am _____

_____

- *Zephaniah 3:17*

God reminds me that I am _____

_____

- *Romans 5:8*

God reminds me that I am _____

_____

Luke 12:6–7

God reminds me that I am _____

_____

1 Peter 2:9

God reminds me that I am _____

_____

Bonus Devotional and Study Guide Days

These serve as deep-dive days, topical encouragements, or personal challenges based on recurring themes across the testimony.

Bonus Day 1: "Your Story Has Power"

Scripture to Read: Revelation 12:11, Psalm 107:2
Key Theme:

"Let the redeemed of the Lord tell their story..." (Psalm 107:2)

Reflection Questions:

What parts of your story have you hidden or been hesitant to share?

_____

_____

Who might be encouraged by the chapters of your life you've walked through with God?

_____

_____

Study Insight: Revelation 12:11 reminds us that we overcome by the blood of the Lamb and the word of our testimony. Sharing your story brings healing not only to others—but to yourself. Your testimony is living proof of God's faithfulness.

Personal Application: Write a 2–3 paragraph version of your testimony. Include a moment of struggle and how God met you there. Ask Him to bring someone into your life who needs to hear what you've lived through.

Bonus Day 2: "Start Again with God"

Scripture to Read: Isaiah 1:18, 2 Corinthians 5:18–19
Key Theme:

"Though your sins are like scarlet, they shall be as white as snow." (Isaiah 1:18)

Reflection Questions:

What moment in your life do you wish you could go back and rewrite?

_____

_____

How does God's mercy make space for new beginnings?

_____

_____

Study Insight: God is in the business of restoration. He doesn't just forgive—He rebuilds. Isaiah 1 reminds us that God can make anything clean. 2 Corinthians 5 emphasizes that we've been given the ministry of reconciliation—because we ourselves were first reconciled.

Personal Application: Think of one area of your life where you want a fresh start. Write a prayer asking God to help you begin again, not in shame, but in grace.

Bonus Day 3: "You Are Not Disqualified"

Scripture to Read: Romans 8:1, Joel 2:25
Key Theme:

"There is now no condemnation for those who are in Christ Jesus."
(Romans 8:1)

Reflection Questions:

Have you ever felt like your past disqualifies you from being used by God?

_____

_____

What truths from Scripture speak louder than your guilt or shame?

_____

_____

Study Insight: Romans 8:1 delivers the powerful truth that there is no condemnation for those in Christ. Joel 2:25 promises restoration of the years the enemy tried to steal. God's grace doesn't ignore your past—it redeems it.

Personal Application: Write a letter to yourself as if God were speaking through you. Remind your heart that you are not disqualified— you are being positioned

Bonus Day 4: "The Light Still Shines in You"

Scripture to Read: John 1:5, Matthew 5:14–16

Key Theme:

"The light shines in the darkness, and the darkness has not overcome it." (John 1:5)

Reflection Questions:

What darkness have you walked through that tried to dim your light?

_____

_____

What helps you remember that God's light in you still shines?

_____

_____

Study Insight: John 1 reminds us that light is stronger than darkness. Matthew 5 calls us to shine our light before others—not perfectly, but authentically. Even when life feels heavy, God's light in us cannot be extinguished.

Personal Application: Light a candle or sit in natural sunlight. Reflect on one way God is still using you, even in your current season. Write it down as a reminder: *His light still shines in me.*

Bonus Day 5: "Grace That Stays"

Scripture to Read: 2 Corinthians 12:9, Hebrews 4:16
Key Theme:

"My grace is sufficient for you, for my power is made perfect in weakness." (2 Corinthians 12:9)

Reflection Questions:

In what areas of life are you feeling weak or weary today?

_____

_____

How has God's grace shown up for you in unexpected ways?

_____

_____

Study Insight: Grace isn't just a one-time rescue—it's the daily strength that carries us through. God invites us in Hebrews 4:16 to approach His throne boldly to receive mercy and find grace to help us when we need it most.

Personal Application: Write a prayer inviting God's grace into your day. List one specific burden you're carrying and ask for His strength to meet you right where you are.

Reflection & Prayer

Reflect: You've walked through a week of devotionals rooted in testimony, scripture, and transformation. As you close this section, remember that your story is still unfolding—and God is the Author. You are a living testimony of grace, growth, and faith. Let this journey affirm your worth and draw you deeper into His presence.

Prayer: Heavenly Father, thank You for being present through each page, each verse, and each whisper of truth. Thank You for the power of transformation and for the testimonies that reflect Your love. Help me to remember who I am in You. Let my life mirror Your grace, and may my story become a light for others. Teach me to live with gratitude, walk in worth, and love boldly—because You first loved me. In Jesus' name, Amen.

Prayer Journal Prompts

Use the following prompts as prayer starters. Let them guide your personal conversations with God as you process what you've read and experienced.

1. Lord, here's what I'm struggling to believe about myself today...

2. Jesus, when I look back at my story, I see You most clearly in this moment...

3. Father, show me how to see myself the way You see me. What do You say about me?

4. God, I'm carrying this burden right now... Will You take it from me and show me peace?

5. Holy Spirit, give me courage to share my testimony with...

6. Today I saw Your grace in...

7. Here's where I need Your light to shine in my life...

8. Help me forgive myself for... and trust You with my healing.

9. Show me someone I can bless today—and help me be bold in doing it.

10. Abba, remind me why I matter. Tell me again that I'm enough. I need to hear it today.

11. God, show me what You're calling me to in this season—and give me the faith to follow.

12. Jesus, what truth do You want to speak over me today that I've been avoiding or forgetting? Take your time.

Write freely. This space in time is between you and God.

Conclusion

A Blessing for the Journey

You've spent the last several days walking through stories of grace, truth, and transformation. You've heard testimonies of faith forged in fire, whispered prayers answered, and identities reclaimed in Christ.

As you've journeyed through these pages, you've walked beside women and men who dared to be honest—about fear, faith, hope, and healing. You've read the moments when they almost gave up and when they chose to keep going. And now, it's your turn.

Now it's your turn to keep walking. Not alone—but hand-in-hand with the God who has never left your side.

Your story doesn't have to be perfect to be powerful. You don't have to have all the answers to be a vessel of truth. You just have to be willing to let God meet you—wherever you are.

Remember this:

- You are not too far behind.

- You are not too broken.

- You are not disqualified.

- You are chosen, seen, loved, and called.

As you step into tomorrow, let these truths go with you:

"The Lord your God is with you, the Mighty Warrior who saves. He will take great delight in you; in His love He will no longer rebuke you, but will rejoice over you with singing." — Zephaniah 3:17

"He who began a good work in you will carry it on to completion until the day of Christ Jesus." — Philippians 1:6

Closing Prayer: Father, thank You for walking with me through every moment—past, present, and future. Thank You for the testimonies that speak life into my own story. Help me to walk boldly in who You've created me to be. Let Your Spirit guide me, and may my life reflect Your light and love every step of the way. In Jesus' name, Amen.

Keep growing. Keep going. Keep shining.

Biographies and how to connect with each of the Co-Authors

Nicky Cuesta

Nicky Cuesta is a dynamic entrepreneur, speaker, bestselling author, and the visionary behind **BALM GLOBAL**—a movement dedicated to empowering women in leadership, business, and personal growth. After leaving corporate America in 2020, Nicky stepped boldly into her purpose, transforming her passion for leadership into a thriving global brand. She is the host of the Building A Leadership Mindset Podcast and the founder of **Ladies of Leadership**, a sisterhood where competition is replaced with collaboration.

A multi-certified coach and community builder, Nicky helps women break free from self-doubt, embrace their worth, and turn their visions into reality. Her journey from corporate limitations to entrepreneurial reign has inspired countless individuals to take risks, rise above challenges, and **own their power**.

With every book, stage, and platform, Nicky's mission remains clear: **to equip, elevate, and empower others to step into their greatness. Connect with Nicky at:**

Website https://www.buildingaleadershipmindset.com/
Facebook https://www.facebook.com/nicky.cuesta
#balmglobal #ladiesofleadership #empowertoinspire

Dr. Oliver T. Reid

 Dr. Reid has published 30 bestselling books, contributed to 17 anthologies, and has won multiple awards for his literary work, including the 2016 IALA Distinction of Excellence Legendary Honoree and NAACP 2016-2017 Black Men Image Award, and Marquise Who's Who Honoree List 2025. Dr. Oliver T. Reid has had the distinct honor of speaking to millions around the world and coaching individuals on four continents. Dr. Reid has been featured on HuffPost, Black Enterprise, ABC, CBS, FOX, NBC, Roku TV, and other international media outlets.

https://drolivertreid.com/

Jose Escobar

Jose Escobar is an award-winning, nationally recognized personal development speaker, 17x plus published author, a sales professional, a dedicated husband, and a proud father of six.

He leads compelling high-level communities consisting of entrepreneurs and advanced leaders through two multi-six-figure business models that have now surpassed 7-figures:
The Entrepreneur's Bookshelf and the Connected Leaders Academy.

Jose's magnetic personality shines in his presentations, where he has reached audiences collectively over 29 million and radiates throughout his dynamic coaching programs, inspiring his international 430+ entrepreneur and executive clientele to master their personal and professional excellence.

His past sales experience led him to amass over $30 million in revenue for the companies he served, and this family man's sales and coaching in the martial arts industry has positively affected the lives of over 500,000 families for the better.

https://www.connectedleadersacademy.com/

 LS Kirkpatrick is an Inspirational Author and Coach for Powerful Purpose. She is an Award Winning Multiple International bestselling author, Award Winning International speaker, a guiding coach and mentor, Podcast host, Editor-in Chief for the magazine, "Wisdom on the Front Porch", wife, mother of 4, grandmother of 15, rancher, 40+ years researching genealogy for many families plus DAR patriots. She gains inspiration from life itself.

"We are all connected through personal encounters, some are brief, others are lifelong relationships."

During the process of learning what it takes to write, publish and market books, she has learned to create positive changes in her clients' writings and business, and find ways to guide their ideas into the reality of their Vision; keeping their voice in what they do, moving forward with their lives in a creative and constructive way.

www.ShineWithLS.com

Reflection Pages

Use these prompts as stand-alone journaling pages or to deepen your experience with any of the devotional days:

What is one truth I've rediscovered about myself through this devotional?

_____

_____

How has God shown up for me this week?

_____

_____

What is a part of my story I feel led to share, and with whom?

_____

_____

What prayer have I seen answered recently?

_____

_____

Where do I feel God stretching my faith next?

_____

_____

Bonus Printables

Scripture Memory Cards

Cut these out or copy them to cards or sticky notes. Keep them visible as daily reminders of God's truth.

"You are the light of the world." Matthew 5:14	*"I praise You because I am fearfully and wonderfully made."* Psalm 139:14
"The Lord will fight for you; you need only to be still." Exodus 14:14	*"My grace is sufficient for you, for My power is made perfect in weakness."* 2 Corinthians 12:9
"Behold, I am doing a new thing..." Isaiah 43:19	*"You are God's masterpiece..."* Ephesians 2:10

Declarations to Speak Over Yourself

Use these as morning declarations or anytime affirmations:

I am loved, chosen, and called by God.	I am enough because Christ lives in me.
My past does not disqualify my future.	I walk in grace, guided by truth.
I am light in the darkness, and hope to the hurting.	I carry purpose. I carry peace. I carry power.

Tape them to your mirror, speak them over your children, or share them with a friend. These are your daily reminders: **You matter. You are becoming. And God is not finished with you yet.**

"You are the light of the world." Matthew 5:14	*"I praise You because I am fearfully and wonderfully made."* Psalm 139:14
"The Lord will fight for you; you need only to be still." Exodus 14:14	*"My grace is sufficient for you, for My power is made perfect in weakness."* 2 Corinthians 12:9
"Behold, I am doing a new thing..." Isaiah 43:19	*"You are God's masterpiece..."* Ephesians 2:10
I am loved, chosen, and called by God.	I am enough because Christ lives in me.
My past does not disqualify my future.	I walk in grace, guided by truth.
I am light in the darkness, and hope to the hurting.	I carry purpose. I carry peace. I carry power.